Original title:
Lacy Outlines Among the Fae Rack

Copyright © 2025 Swan Charm
All rights reserved.

Author: Kätriin Kaldaru
ISBN HARDBACK: 978-1-80559-450-5
ISBN PAPERBACK: 978-1-80559-949-4

Faerie-Threaded Echoes in Nature's Heart

In twilight glow, the faeries dance,
With whispers soft, they weave romance.
Among the trees, their laughter sings,
As nature sways, and each heart springs.

Beneath the moon, a silver thread,
Where magic flows, the world is fed.
In gentle streams, the secrets flow,
Their glimmers bright, in night's soft glow.

Through petals fair, their tales are spun,
In whispers sweet, they've just begun.
The world alive with every breeze,
Through verdant woods and ancient trees.

In every shadow, light shall twine,
With melodies that gently shine.
The faerie gifts, both wild and free,
Umbrace the heart of you and me.

With every rustle, echoes play,
In nature's heart, they find their way.
A timeless bond, in blissful trance,
In faerie-threaded, bold romance.

Delicate Patterns in the Moonlight

Silver beams dance on quiet seas,
Whispers of night carried by the breeze.
Shadows play in the gentle glow,
Secrets shared where the soft winds blow.

Pale reflections on silken waves,
Tales of dreams that the night time saves.
Each ripple tells a story so sweet,
Echoing soft in the night's heartbeat.

A canvas stretches from shore to star,
Painted moments, both near and far.
Nestled softly in twilight's embrace,
Where time suspends in a hushed space.

Celestial Filigree Adrift in Air

Gleaming threads weave through the night,
Delicate patterns shaped by light.
Every twinkle a story told,
Woven in silver, spun from gold.

Stars dip gently like notes in song,
Melodies drifting where dreams belong.
Whispers of magic drift on high,
In the vast tapestry of the sky.

Floating softly like feathers bright,
Carried onward by the cool night.
Each breath of air a gentle sigh,
As the cosmos breathes, we wonder why.

Threads of Fantasy Beneath the Stars

In the hush of night, fantasies bloom,
Under the stars, dispelling gloom.
Threaded dreams in the fabric of dark,
Flickering softly, igniting a spark.

Each shining point a wish on a flight,
Guiding the hearts lost in their plight.
Weaving tales in the celestial expanse,
Drawn to the dance of a heavenly chance.

Mosaics glimmer, a playful show,
Inviting souls to wander and glow.
In the vastness, a promise to keep,
With each thread woven, we gently leap.

Mystical Lace on Whispering Winds

Lace-like whispers ride on the breeze,
Intricate patterns of rustling leaves.
They tell of secrets tucked far away,
In echoes and sighs where shadows play.

Softly they twirl in the cool night air,
Dancing lightly with elegant flair.
Each gentle gust carries a tune,
Sung by the heart of the silvery moon.

Fleeting whispers, a tender embrace,
Binding our dreams in the night's gentle grace.
In the twilight's kiss, we find our song,
With mystical lace, where we belong.

Whispers of Gossamer Dreams

In a garden where silence breathes,
Soft petals brush against the night,
Dreams entwined in moonlit weaves,
Whispers dance, elusive and light.

Stars above, like eyes that gleam,
Veils of hope in twilight's grasp,
Each flicker speaks a quiet theme,
Holding hearts in gentle clasp.

Morning dew, a fragile chance,
Catching secrets in its sheen,
With every shimmer, a fleeting glance,
Of all the magic that has been.

Clouds drift lightly, shadows play,
Brush of colors, soft and pale,
In the dawn, dreams fade away,
Yet their echoes still prevail.

A journey through the soul's abode,
Where every whisper tells a tale,
In gossamer, the past bestowed,
Love's essence will always sail.

Shadows Woven in Elven Threads

Beneath the canopy of leaves,
Where light and shadow intertwine,
Ancient songs the forest weaves,
In whispers shared by spirits fine.

Silken threads of gold and green,
Stitch the night with tales untold,
In hidden paths where we convene,
Embers flicker, softly bold.

Moonlit glades, where faeries tread,
One can hear the laughter play,
In every turn, a story spread,
Time slips softly, fades away.

Branches bow to secrets kept,
Tales of old entwined in time,
A tapestry where dreams have crept,
Our hearts bound in silent rhyme.

Thus, in twilight's gentle sway,
Elven threads weave through the air,
In shadows deep where spirits stay,
A world beyond, fragile and rare.

The Veil of Twilight's Embrace

At dusk, the sky wears softest gowns,
Hues of lavender and rose,
As day relinquishes its crowns,
To night, where hidden magic grows.

With each breath, the world draws near,
In shadows deep, the spirit flies,
Indistinct whispers, keen yet clear,
Revealing truths in twilight skies.

The veil hangs low, so silky thin,
Between the worlds we dare to dream,
In every heart, a spark within,
Illuminated by moonbeam.

Stars awaken, glimmer bright,
In their glow, our wishes soar,
In this realm, we find our light,
Past the veil, we are much more.

Embrace the night, relinquish fears,
In the silence, we belong,
Through whispered wishes, we are near,
The twilight beckons us along.

Enchanted Traces of Ethereal Dance

In glimmers soft where shadows play,
The moon invites a silent trance,
Around soft hills, they sway and sway,
In rhythm's pulse, a timeless dance.

Each step is light, a whispering breeze,
As stars shimmer, a twinkling chance,
A tapestry of echoes pleases,
Awakening our hearts to prance.

Gossamer threads of worn delight,
Entwine the memories we hold dear,
In every twirl, a spark ignites,
A dance that draws us ever near.

With laughter soft as petals fall,
We glide through realms where dreams expand,
In this enchanted, timeless hall,
We lose ourselves, as destinies blend.

Each moment draped in starlit grace,
A fleeting glimpse of what may be,
In the dance, we find our place,
Ethereal traces, wild and free.

Ephemeral Stitches in the Meadow's Heart

In fields where wildflowers sway,
Threads of sunlight softly play,
Each blossom a fleeting breath,
Whispering tales of life and death.

Colors dance in the gentle breeze,
Nature's fabric never ceases,
Stitched in moments, brief and bright,
Fading fast, like day to night.

Bees hum softly, weaving sweet,
In harmony, they find their beat,
While shadows stretch, the sun descends,
A fleeting touch that never ends.

Softly the winds begin to sigh,
As dusk wraps the meadow high,
Ephemeral, the beauty lies,
In the transient, time swiftly flies.

Yet in our hearts, they leave their mark,
These stitches bright against the dark,
A memory of blooms once seen,
In the meadow's heart, a dream serene.

The Ethereal Weave of Faery Lore

In twilight's glow, where shadows linger,
Whispers dance on softest finger,
Threads of magic in the air,
Woven tales of faeries fair.

They flit beneath the silver moon,
Singing soft an ancient tune,
With every note, the night does spark,
Where dreams unfurl and secrets mark.

Delicate wings brush through the leaves,
Ancient stories the heart believes,
In the stillness, echoes call,
Enchanting spells that rise and fall.

Each dew drop glistens with their plight,
Caught in starlight, pure and bright,
The weave of faery, soft yet bold,
In every tale, a treasure told.

Even as dawn begins to break,
The faery's essence we still take,
For in the heart, their lore remains,
A silken thread in truth's domains.

Enchantment's Brush in the Hollow's Embrace

In a hollow where shadows play,
Enchantment weaves the night and day,
A brush of air, a lover's sigh,
Lifting spirits, soaring high.

Whispers carry on the breeze,
Banishing doubts with gentle ease,
Where ancient trees stand guard and watch,
Beneath their boughs, the heart does catch.

Every leaf reflects a dream,
In nature's arms, life's sweet esteem,
The brush of enchantment dances near,
A fleeting moment, crystal clear.

Through veils of mist, stories unfold,
In this embrace, the magic's bold,
With every step on mossy floor,
The heartbeats echo, evermore.

Held in the hollow, soft and bright,
Where daydreams linger, pure delight,
A gentle touch, a world awakes,
In enchantment's brush, the spirit shakes.

Twilight Tangles of Nature's Heart

When dusk approaches, shadows blend,
The twilight tangles, dreams descend,
Nature's heart beats slow and deep,
In quiet moments, we still keep.

Fibers of night in shades of gray,
Embracing thoughts that softly sway,
Whispers of the day's retreat,
In every pulse, a rhythm sweet.

Stars ignite in velvet skies,
Glimmers of hope in a night's eyes,
Nature calls with a siren's song,
Inviting souls where they belong.

With every rustle, every sigh,
The universe stretches wide and high,
Tangled dreams in the moon's embrace,
Guide the heart to its rightful place.

As darkness blooms, a magic seen,
In twinkling stars, a silver sheen,
Tangled in nature's vast domain,
Where light and shadow dance, remain.

Moonlit Patterns Among the Whispering Trees

Under the moon's soft glow, they sway,
Branches dance in the twilight play.
Silvery shadows cast on the ground,
Secrets of the night, silence profound.

Stars twinkle high in the velvet air,
While whispers of leaves tell tales rare.
Cool breezes hum a lullaby tune,
Nature's magic unfolds in the moon.

The ground beneath is a tapestry woven,
With patterns of dreams that remain unspoken.
Cool dew plants kisses on blades of grass,
As time drifts slowly, hours do pass.

Owls call out with wisdom of night,
Guardians of stories hidden from sight.
Each rustle and murmur becomes a song,
In this sacred space where hearts belong.

Memories linger in every breath,
In the hush of the woods, beyond death.
With each gentle sway and each silent plea,
Moonlit patterns weave through the trees.

The Spectral Weave of Nature's Charm

In the heart of the glade, colors blend,
Nature's artistry, a timeless friend.
Petals flutter softly in cool twilight,
Unraveling beauty, hidden from sight.

Each leaf a whisper, each blossom a dream,
Flowing like rivers through a gentle stream.
Among the shadows, where secrets ignite,
Nature's charm dances in the soft light.

Beneath the canopy, tales intertwined,
Echoes of life in the stillness confined.
The breeze carries laughter, spirits arise,
In the gentle rustle, hear nature's sighs.

Misty mornings bring wonders anew,
Every sunrise paints a vibrant hue.
In the depths of the forest, mysteries loom,
Spectral weaves bloom in the forest's room.

With the night's embrace, dreams now ignite,
Each twinkling star, a flicker of light.
Nature's charm lingers, a soft gentle balm,
Woven together, a spell so disarm.

Ties of Wonder in the Leafy Shadows

In the leafy shadows, wonders awake,
Nature's whispers dance, ripples they make.
Each branch a story, each stone a sage,
Ties of wonder weave through each age.

Crisp air carries scents so divine,
Like memories tied to the twisting vine.
The play of light in the emerald hues,
Bathed in magic, the heart renews.

Velvet evenings, where fireflies dwell,
Glow like messages too sweet to tell.
They flicker and glow, a celestial show,
Drawing us closer to the secrets below.

Soft echoes of laughter, a fleeting caress,
Bring forth the beauty, nature's finesse.
In shadows we find what daylight won't show,
Ties of wonder in the moon's gentle flow.

As night's blanket wraps the earth tight,
Dreams take flight, and spirits unite.
In the tranquil embrace, we remain entranced,
In the ties of wonder, our hearts stolen, danced.

Secrets Wrapped in Forest's Embrace

In midnight's cloak, secrets reside,
Wrapped in whispers where shadows hide.
Every rustling leaf holds a tale,
Songs of the forest, a timeless veil.

Old trunks stand proud with wisdom to share,
Tales of journeys held in their care.
The moonlight weaves through the branches so brave,
Singing softly over each mossy grave.

Twilight beckons, a call to explore,
Mysteries linger behind every door.
An owl's gentle hoot, the night's own sound,
Encircles us, pulls us deeper, profound.

Amidst the ferns and wildflower blooms,
Secrets awaken in nature's wombs.
Each step we take, a new path to trace,
Finding solace in the forest's embrace.

In the quietude, our spirits align,
Discovering tales, both yours and mine.
Together we wander, hands intertwined,
In the secrets wrapped, our hearts refined.

Ephemeral Glances Among Enchanted Ferns

In the woods of whispers low,
Ferns sway gently, secrets flow.
A fleeting glance, a moment's grace,
Nature's beauty, a soft embrace.

Sunlight dapples, shadows weave,
Among the leaves, we dare believe.
An ephemeral dance, so sweet and fair,
Captured glances in the fresh cool air.

With every breeze, a story breathes,
A tender touch in emerald leaves.
Ferns that flutter, hearts untold,
Revealing magic in green and gold.

Misty morns give dreams a chance,
Ephemeral worlds in woodland dance.
In the hush, we find our way,
Among enchanted ferns, we stay.

In joyful silence, time stands still,
Amidst the ferns, we find our thrill.
A moment precious, forever lost,
Ephemeral glances, we pay the cost.

The Lattice of Faerie Light and Shadow

In twilight's glow, the faeries play,
Dancing in shadows, fading away.
A lattice of light where dreams unfold,
Secrets whispered, stories told.

Glints of magic through the trees,
Echoes of laughter on the breeze.
In the glimmer, shadows intertwine,
Twinkling stars in a frame divine.

Patterns woven, soft and bright,
The faerie realm, a wondrous sight.
With every flicker, a spell is cast,
Time dissolving, moments past.

Under the moon, the world transforms,
In the dance where magic warms.
Lost in wonder, lost in glee,
The lattice of shadows calls to me.

Through veils of light, the night does weave,
In faerie realms, we dare believe.
Caught in the beauty, lost in the play,
Forever enchanted, we long to stay.

Outlines of Dreams Among the Blossoms

Beneath the blooms of vibrant hue,
Dreams take shape, both fresh and new.
Butterflies dance in the softest light,
Sketching visions, taking flight.

Petals whisper secrets soft,
In fragrant dreams, we drift aloft.
Glimmers of hope in every shade,
Outline of tomorrow, gently laid.

Amidst the blossoms, life unfolds,
In colors bright, each story told.
With every gust, our wishes soar,
Among the flowers, we seek for more.

A garden lush, a world divine,
Where hearts entwine, and spirits shine.
In outlines of dreams, we find our way,
Comfort and beauty in bright array.

A tapestry woven from nature's thread,
In the dance of blooms, our hopes are fed.
Among the blossoms, forever we'll dwell,
In fragile beauty, we weave our spell.

Mysteries of the Moonlit Wonderland

Under the moon's soft, silver gaze,
A wonderland of hidden ways.
Mysteries float on a silken breeze,
Awakening dreams beneath the trees.

In shadows deep, secrets unfold,
Whispers of magic, tales of old.
The night ignites with shimmering light,
A realm of wonder, pure delight.

Glimmers dance on the water's face,
In moonlit whispers, we find our place.
With every star a story spun,
In this vast world, we are all one.

A symphony plays in the cool night air,
Echoing softly, a song of care.
In moonlight's glow, our hearts embrace,
The mysteries that time cannot erase.

So let the night take us away,
In this wonderland, forever we'll stay.
From shadows deep to the brightest part,
In moonlit magic, we find our heart.

Mists that Cloak the Woodland Secrets

Mists roll in with whispering grace,
Veils that hide, a soft embrace.
Trees stand guard, ancient and wise,
Secrets shimmer under starry skies.

Footsteps soft on mossy ground,
Nature's breath, a tranquil sound.
Shadows dance in twilight's glow,
Misty realms where few may go.

A fox slips by with cautious pride,
In the hush where echoes bide.
Hidden paths weave tales untold,
In the woods where dreams unfold.

Leaves rustle, a fleeting sigh,
With every turn, the spirits fly.
Clocks of time in silence keep,
Awakening the woods from sleep.

In twilight hours, mysteries reign,
Each breath a song, both sweet and plain.
Mists that cloak the woodland's heart,
In every shadow, secrets start.

Gossamer Wings in the Twilight

Gossamer wings on winds of night,
Emerge from shadows, soft and light.
They flutter by, a fleeting sight,
In hues that dance with fading light.

Moonbeams kiss the flowers' heads,
Whispers weave where silence spreads.
The air is filled with magic's tune,
Underneath the watchful moon.

A tapestry of starlit dreams,
Weaving through the silver beams.
Every flitter, an artist's brush,
In the dusk, a gentle hush.

With every beat, a story told,
Of love and wonder, brave and bold.
Boundless journeys, soft and sweet,
In twilight's fold, the worlds compete.

So let us drift on evening's sails,
With gossamer wings and whispered trails.
In twilight's arms, we find our flight,
Embraced by magic, lost in night.

The Hidden Artistry of Wandering Souls

Wandering souls in unknown lands,
Tracing paths with gentle hands.
Each step a brush upon the earth,
Painting stories of joy and mirth.

Beneath the sky, vast and wide,
The heartbeats echo, spirits guide.
In every glance, a spark ignites,
A tapestry spun from starlit nights.

Laughter lingers in the air,
Wisps of dreams escape with flair.
Every journey a work of art,
The road ahead, a brand new start.

Through valleys deep and mountains high,
Under the canvas of the sky.
Together they weave, intertwine,
The hidden artistry of time.

So let us wander, free and bold,
With whispered tales of love retold.
In every step, let souls unite,
In a dance of shadows and of light.

Radiant Traces in the Fae Light

Radiant traces shimmer bright,
Dancing softly in the night.
Fae light flickers, shadows play,
Guiding dreamers on their way.

In the glade where wishes bloom,
Magic brews within the gloom.
Every sparkle, a tender sigh,
In the twilight, spirits fly.

Whispers echo, secrets shared,
A world enchanted, none compared.
With every step upon the glen,
We find ourselves in realms again.

Glimmers weave through ancient trees,
A symphony on the evening breeze.
With radiant traces, hearts ignite,
In the embrace of fae light.

So linger long in twilight's grace,
Let the magic find its place.
In the night where wonders call,
Radiant traces guide us all.

Delicate Patterns of Forgotten Realms

In twilight's breath, the shadows weave,
A dance of dreams where whispers cleave.
Forgotten realms, in silence bloom,
Their secrets bound in twilight's loom.

Dew-kissed petals, soft and frail,
Echo stories of ancient trails.
Threads of silver, glimmers bright,
Guide the lost through endless night.

In hidden nooks, the echoes sigh,
Where time stands still, and spirits fly.
Patterns sketch the tales once told,
In memories wrapped, like threads of gold.

Veils of mist, both soft and deep,
Guard the dreams that gently sleep.
Each fading echo, a heart's refrain,
In delicate patterns, they remain.

Through veils of time, we wander free,
In realms forgotten, we long to see.
The dance of shadows, a timeless flame,
In delicate patterns, call our name.

Ethereal Whispers in the Glade

Beneath the boughs where silence sings,
Ethereal whispers on gentle wings.
Secrets rustle with each soft breeze,
In the glade's heart, the world finds peace.

Luminous orbs in twilight glow,
Guide the lost to where magic flows.
Where shadows play and spirits roam,
In the glade's embrace, we find our home.

Fleeting moments, like mist they rise,
Twinkling lights in starlit skies.
Each whisper carries a soul's desire,
In the hush of night, we spark the fire.

Colors dance in a soft array,
Painting tales of night and day.
In every breath, the glade confides,
The beauty found where the heart abides.

As dawn breaks through the leafy veil,
Ethereal echoes in the pale,
With every step, we weave the song,
In whispers sweet, where we belong.

Tapestries of Enchantment

In twilight threads, a tale is spun,
Tapestries weave where dreams are won.
Colors blend in a dance divine,
In every stitch, a star will shine.

Woven whispers beneath the moon,
Echo softly, a haunting tune.
Fables linger in the golden light,
In enchanted threads, we take flight.

Each fabric holds a world apart,
Embroidered visions, a fragile heart.
Patterns swirl in a playful way,
Guiding souls on their winding way.

With every knot, a story told,
Of bravery, love, and hearts so bold.
Threads of fate pull and entwine,
In tapestries rich, our dreams align.

As daylight fades and shadows blend,
Enchantment flows, it will not end.
In every weave, our spirits soar,
In tapestries, we seek for more.

Shadowed Petals and Hidden Paths

In gardens vast, where shadows lie,
Petals whisper, secrets sigh.
Hidden paths in twilight's blush,
Softly calling in the hush.

Through winding trails, we drift along,
Every step, a whispered song.
Fragments of the night embrace,
In shadowed petals, we find grace.

Moonlit glimmers on dew-kissed leaves,
Stories woven, like mystical weaves.
Each hidden path a journey's start,
In every turn, a beating heart.

Flickering lights in the dusky gloom,
Guide the way, dispel the doom.
Nature's wonders, vast and deep,
In shadowed petals, secrets keep.

As dawn approaches, shadows fade,
Yet in our hearts, the beauty stayed.
Forever woven, the paths we tread,
In shadowed petals, dreams are fed.

Wandering Among the Weavings of Dreams

In twilight's glow, I softly tread,
Where whispers weave through night's soft thread.
Each shadow dances, a silent sway,
Guiding me through the dreams that play.

Stars alight with stories to share,
The cosmos cradles my thoughts in prayer.
I trace the paths of forgotten lore,
As starlit echoes call me to explore.

The moon's embrace, a gentle guide,
Through shimmering veils, I wander wide.
Each breath a tapestry, rich and deep,
In the realm of dreams, my heart will leap.

A chorus of visions, woven tight,
In every corner of the mystic night.
With every step, the dreamscape swells,
A journey into where wonder dwells.

With dawn's first light, my visions fade,
Yet in my heart, the dreams have stayed.
Wandering still, I hold them near,
The weavings of dreams, forever clear.

Elusive Embroidery of Nature's Heart

In forest depths where silence sings,
The whispers of the earth take wings.
With every leaf and dew-kissed blade,
Nature's heart in art displayed.

A canvas rich with vibrant hues,
Colors dance in morning's dew.
Elusive threads of life entwine,
Embroidering the woods divine.

The rivers weave their winding tales,
As breezes carry fragrant gales.
Each creature paints a story bright,
In harmony, they share their light.

Misty veils caress the dawn,
As daylight breaks, the shadows yawn.
In the symphony of nature's song,
I find a place where I belong.

With every step on verdant ground,
In nature's heart, my soul is found.
The embroidery of life so fine,
A tapestry that's yours and mine.

Flight of the Aetherial Spiders

Above the world, the spiders soar,
With silken wings, they weave and explore.
In twilight's glow, they dance with grace,
A ballet spun in ethereal space.

Each thread of light, a story spun,
A gossamer trail, where dreams become.
They cast their nets of glimmering dew,
Catching moments, both old and new.

With whispers soft and whispers sweet,
They beckon the night with nimble feet.
In the cool embrace of moonlit skies,
Aetherial spiders, where magic lies.

They spin their webs, a fragile art,
Binding the universe with a tender heart.
As dawn approaches, they take their flight,
Fading gently into morning light.

Yet in the stillness, their patterns stay,
In every heart, a trace of play.
Flight of the spiders, swift and free,
A reminder of the dreams we see.

Imprints of Magic on the Forest Floor

In the soft embrace of ancient trees,
Where whispers dance upon the breeze.
Magic lingers in the air,
Imprints left with gentle care.

Mushrooms sprout with colors bright,
Sprinkling joy in the cloak of night.
Footprints trace the faerie's roam,
Each path a heart that calls this home.

Beneath the ferns, secrets hide,
In sunlit glades, where dreams abide.
Every stone, a tale to tell,
Of magic woven, where shadows dwell.

With every rustle, stories bloom,
Nature whispers, dispelling gloom.
The forest holds a sacred lore,
Imprints of magic forevermore.

As twilight falls, the enchantment's clear,
In the forest's heart, magic draws near.
With every step, I'm forever changed,
Imprints of magic, forever ranged.

Secrets of the Enchanted Canopy

Beneath the leaves, whispers call,
Where shadows dance and raindrops fall.
Ancient trees with stories weave,
In their arms, the secrets cleave.

Twinkling lights in twilight's embrace,
Guiding footsteps through time and space.
Mysterious paths, oh so rare,
Lead to magic hidden there.

In cool moss beds, dreams take flight,
While stars peek through the veil of night.
Silent oaths the boughs bestow,
Songs of wonder softly flow.

Crickets chirp a gentle tune,
As moonbeams spin a silver rune.
Each rustling leaf holds a prayer,
In this realm of whispered air.

Here in the shadows we remain,
Sipping dew like sweet champagne.
Beneath the canopy's spray,
Secrets linger, night and day.

Dappled Moonlight and Faerie Dews

In the hush of a dawning day,
Moonlight dances in a shimmering play.
Dewdrops cling to emerald blades,
A symphony in the glade.

Soft whispers float on the breeze,
Carrying tales from ancient trees.
Faerie lights blink and glide,
In this realm where dreams reside.

Night flowers bloom in softest hue,
Under the watchful gaze of dew.
Silk-like threads of luminous white,
Weave through shadows, pure delight.

Crickets sing their lullaby sweet,
Echoing through the forest's beat.
With every pulse, the heart does sway,
In moonlit magic, night's ballet.

Hold your breath as dreams unfold,
In the twilight, stories told.
Each shimmer a glimpse divine,
In the light where faeries shine.

Threads of Wonder in Faerie Light

In the thicket where wishes ride,
Threads of wonder gently glide.
Luminous trails, a sparkling path,
To the heart of the faerie bath.

With every glance, a secret hum,
Wrapped in stillness, soft and numb.
Shadows twine with morning's bloom,
In the depths of the forest's room.

Silvery webs of heart's pure song,
Guide the way where dreams belong.
In the hush, the unseen stirs,
Calling forth the song of furs.

Dancing motes, the air alive,
With magic where spirit thrives.
Threads entwined in a vibrant haze,
Weaving through enchanted days.

In this realm where wishes soar,
Every heartbeat echoes more.
Alive with tales of timeless nights,
In the web of faerie lights.

Illusions in the Verdant Hollow

In the hollow where shadows blend,
Illusions twist and softly bend.
Brambles whisper secrets old,
Wrapped in dreams and wonder bold.

Underfoot, the soft moss glows,
A carpet where the moonlight flows.
Each rustling leaf a fleeting thought,
In the web of magic, caught.

Night blooms pulse with a gentle sigh,
As stars drape their fabric high.
In this maze of nature's art,
Illusions cradle every heart.

Echoes linger in the air,
Memories drift without a care.
Through the mist, soft shadows play,
In the verdant hollow's sway.

Ready to dance with the unknown,
Through tangled paths, we have grown.
In this realm where visions swell,
Secrets weave their silvery spell.

Patterns of Joy Beneath the Faery Sky

In twilight's hue, the colors dance,
Each whispering breeze, a soft romance.
Petals twirl in laughter's glow,
A tapestry of joy, we sow.

Moonlit trails, where shadows play,
Secrets held in soft array.
Joy unfurls in every sigh,
Beneath the realms where faeries fly.

Glimmers sprout on emerald leaves,
In every heart, the magic weaves.
The stars above begin to sing,
As whispers of delight take wing.

Colors burst in joyful streams,
Each moment stitched with silver seams.
Patterns of joy entwine the night,
As faery dreams take their flight.

In the silence, a soft embrace,
Nature hums in gentle grace.
Through every step, a dance unfolds,
Beneath the faery sky, so bold.

The Hidden Threads of Magical Whispers

In hidden nooks where shadows dwell,
Secrets weave a silent spell.
Voices soft as misty breeze,
Whisper tales among the trees.

Twilight secrets softly spun,
In golden light, magic's begun.
Each thread a story, delicate, rare,
Hiding wonders floating in air.

Glimmering paths of silken lace,
Invite us to a sacred space.
With every heartbeat, whispers draw,
Unseen patterns that inspire awe.

Chasing echoes, we entwine,
With every whisper, the stars align.
Hidden threads of night and day,
In gentle hands, they gently sway.

As dreams unfold in secret streams,
The world awakens from its dreams.
Threads of magic, soft and bright,
Guide us through the starry night.

Mystical Trails in the Forest's Embrace

In the forest's arms, we roam free,
Where ancient trees whisper to thee.
Sunbeams weave through branches high,
Creating paths where spirits lie.

Each step measures the earth's sweet song,
With nature's pulse, we feel we belong.
Mystical trails with secrets hold,
Stories of wanderers, wise and bold.

Covered in ferns, the shadows creep,
In mossy beds, the wild dreams sleep.
The forest breathes, and we in turn,
Stoke the flame of wanderlust's burn.

The scent of pine and earthy clay,
Guide the heart along the way.
Mystical threads in every glance,
Awake a world where spirits dance.

As twilight descends in hues of gold,
The stories of the forest unfold.
In this embrace, we find our place,
Amongst the whispers, love, and grace.

Starlit Caresses in the Ferny Underbush

Beneath the stars, a world divine,
In ferny nooks, our hearts entwine.
With each caress of night's cool breeze,
The gentle touch of memories.

Silhouettes dance in moon's soft glow,
As starlit whispers gently flow.
Every shadow tells a tale,
In hidden realms where dreams prevail.

The underbush, a cozy nest,
Where fantasies are born and rest.
Each star above, a guiding light,
In this embrace, the soul takes flight.

Swaying ferns in rhythmic time,
In harmony, they softly chime.
Starlit caresses, dreams ascend,
In nature's cradle, hearts will mend.

The night wraps us in tender care,
In every breath, the magic's there.
Beneath the stars, we linger still,
In ferny dreams, the heart we fill.

Fractals of Delight in the Fae Realm

In twilight hues where fairies dance,
Soft glimmers spin in twirling chance.
Mushrooms glow beneath the trees,
Their laughter mingles with the breeze.

Petals shimmer, secrets shared,
In a world where none are scared.
Each moment sparks with radiant light,
Creating dreams that take to flight.

Winding paths of emerald lace,
Lead to realms in hidden space.
Where wishes bloom on every vine,
And hearts unite in sweet divine.

The air hums with a magic song,
In this realm, we all belong.
With every flutter, joy ignites,
Within fractals of dazzling sights.

From dusk till dawn, the stories weave,
In the spaces where we believe.
For in this land of endless delight,
Hope springs forth like stars at night.

The Subtle Weaving of Nature's Dreams

In soft embrace of morning light,
Nature weaves her dreams in flight.
Threads of green and skies of blue,
Whispers weave the world anew.

Each petal drops a tale untold,
In colors bright and shades of gold.
Leaves unfurl like secrets shared,
In the quiet, hearts are bared.

The rivers flow with gentle grace,
Reflecting time in every space.
Echoes of the past reside,
In the currents that abide.

From mountains high to valleys low,
Nature hums a soft arpeggio.
Each creature plays a note so sweet,
In the symphony beneath our feet.

With every dawn, a new refrain,
In nature's dreams, we find our gain.
The subtle weaving never ends,
As time and beauty intertwine, my friends.

Secrets Beneath the Whispering Leaves

Beneath the leaves where shadows play,
Secrets linger and gently sway.
The breeze carries tales untold,
In rustling whispers, mysteries unfold.

The roots of trees, they stretch and yearn,
In silent thoughts, old stories burn.
Each rustle holds an ancient truth,
Guarded close, the essence of youth.

The dappled light paints patterns bold,
As time weaves knots both new and old.
In the forest's heart, secrets bloom,
Filling the air, the sweet perfume.

Amid the petals, soft and frail,
Lie memories wrapped in nature's veil.
The sun will dance, the shadows shift,
As every leaf becomes a gift.

So lean in close, embrace the sound,
For in this hush, the truth is found.
With every whisper, a tale will weave,
Secrets bound deep beneath the leaves.

Echoes of the Enchanted Boughs

In the heart of groves where echoes dwell,
The boughs weave stories, casting a spell.
Each branch extends like a caring hand,
Offering shade in this magical land.

The rustling leaves hum a soft tune,
While twilight dances, kissed by the moon.
Branches cradle secrets from the past,
Echoes of laughter, holding steadfast.

With every sway, the stories blend,
In whispered voices, they never end.
The bark is worn with the weight of time,
Each groove a verse in nature's rhyme.

Birds flit about, sharing their songs,
In this world where each note belongs.
From dusk till dawn, the boughs will sing,
Of the beauty each season brings.

So wander here, where the wild things roam,
Among the echoes, you'll find your home.
For in the dance of the rustling leaves,
Lie the secrets of magic that never leaves.

Tapestries of the Enchanted Realm

In twilight's gleam, the shadows wove,
Whispers dance in the forest grove.
Starlit dreams weave tales anew,
In the heart of night, they break through.

Ancient trees, with secrets clasped,
Hold the wisdom of ages grasped.
Each leaf a story, every breeze,
Echoes of magic beneath the trees.

The moonlight spills like liquid gold,
Crafting tales that never grow old.
A symphony of nature's art,
Tapestries that warm the heart.

Through paths unseen, we wander deep,
In the embrace where shadows creep.
Mysteries twine in every step,
The realm enchants, and we are kept.

Threads of light in every glen,
Bind the memories of once and then.
In this haven of soft embrace,
Time dissolves, leaving no trace.

Flickering Threads of the Unknown

Beneath the surface, shadows stir,
Secrets flicker, dreams whisper.
Paths untamed, where spirits roam,
In the darkness, we find a home.

Whirling colors in the night,
Illuminate with fleeting light.
Each heartbeat echoes through the void,
Mysteries live where dreams have toyed.

Tangled webs of twilight's art,
Dancing visions, worlds depart.
Through the fog, we seek to find,
The flickering threads of the mind.

Echoes of laughter, sighs of fear,
All converge when the end is near.
In the shimmer of what may be,
Life unveils its mystery.

Each step forward, a leap of faith,
Into the dark, embracing fate.
The unknown calls, a siren's song,
Flickering threads, where we belong.

A Dance of Silken Echoes

In the stillness, soft whispers play,
Silken echoes guide our way.
Twilight's touch on gentle air,
A dance unfolds, beyond compare.

With every heartbeat, shadows twirl,
Secrets held in a timeless swirl.
Where wishes weave and dreams ignite,
We glide through realms bathed in light.

Delicate patterns, grace takes flight,
In this moment, we unite.
Suspended in the breath of time,
Melodies rise, soft and sublime.

Every note a story spun,
In the night, all hearts are one.
Fleeting glimpses, tender and bright,
Ribbons of joy in endless night.

As stars twinkle, we draw near,
In this symphony, nothing to fear.
A dance of echoes, forever free,
Silken shadows, you and me.

The Hidden Patterns of Wandering Lights

Among the trees, soft glimmers sway,
Wandering lights lead hearts astray.
Crimson and gold in twilight's tune,
A secret language beneath the moon.

In night's embrace, we uncover threads,
Stories linger where silence spreads.
Each flicker a promise, bold and bright,
Illuminating the edges of night.

Through valleys deep, and mountains high,
Patterns dance beneath the sky.
With every pulse, the stars collide,
Guiding souls like a gentle tide.

The echoes' call, a soft caress,
In hidden paths, we find our rest.
Spirits whisper, drawing near,
In the chaos, we sense no fear.

As wandering lights begin to fade,
We follow courage, unafraid.
For in the darkness, we find our sight,
The hidden patterns of the night.

Captivating Weave Beneath the ancient Canopy

In twilight's grasp, the shadows sigh,
Whispers weave through branches high.
Nature's tale, a silent song,
As stars emerge, night lingers long.

Moonlit paths where secrets lay,
Glimmers guide the wandering way.
Every leaf a story holds,
In this realm, the magic unfolds.

The breeze, a thread of mystic lore,
Calls forth spirits from days of yore.
Dancing lights, like fireflies flick,
Entwined in dreams, the heartbeats quick.

Veils of mist, enchanting sights,
Ignite the dances of velvet nights.
Cloaked in wonder, the forest sways,
Capturing souls in its gentle maze.

Here beneath the ageless trees,
Time stands still, a tranquil ease.
In this haven, lost yet found,
Life's tapestry spins profound.

Echoes of the Enchantress's Dance

Amidst the glades, the shadows twirl,
An enchantress spins, a silken furl.
Her laughter rings like silver chime,
Each movement flows, defying time.

Moonbeams trace her graceful form,
In the night's embrace, a silent storm.
With every step, the earth awakes,
As ancient magic softly breaks.

Veils of light entwine and weave,
In this dreamscape, none can leave.
Her eyes, deep wells of starry bright,
Captivate the hearts in flight.

Around her realm, dreams intertwine,
Beauty blossoms in the pine.
Echoes whisper of love's sweet trance,
Lost in the rhythm of the dance.

A tapestry of night and flame,
Every heartbeat calls her name.
In shadows deep, her spirit prays,
To guide the lost through endless ways.

Shadows of Elegance in Ethereal Woods

In twilight's fold, the shadows play,
Draped in elegance, night holds sway.
Each rustling leaf a soft refrain,
As whispered dreams descend like rain.

The willow weeps, its branches low,
Caressing secrets only she knows.
Misty tendrils veil the air,
A dance of spirits hidden there.

Moonlit glimmers on the stream,
Reflecting tales that softly beam.
In this realm of twilight grace,
Wonders fade in time's embrace.

Footsteps echo, soft and light,
Through ethereal woods, kissed by night.
A ballet spun on nature's thread,
Where every heartbeat, gently led.

Shadows twine in gentle sway,
Fleeting moments slip away.
Ephemeral beauty, forever drawn,
In the silence, the night moves on.

Gleams and Glimmers of Forgotten Dreams

In the attic of time, dust collects,
Memories lost, ancient effects.
Gleams of laughter echo faint,
Whispers of dreams paint without a taint.

Faded pictures, treasures rare,
Spark imaginations unaware.
Every glance, a tale unfolds,
In shadows of time, the heart beholds.

Glimmers dance on the edge of night,
Awakening visions dimmed from sight.
Floating softly like a song,
Inviting souls where they belong.

Forgotten dreams, like morning dew,
Hope rekindles, fresh and new.
In stillness lies the promise clear,
Of adventures waiting, drawing near.

Through the layers of dust and time,
Each heartbeat whispers, a gentle chime.
In this realm where night redeems,
We find the beauty of forgotten dreams.

The Luminance of the Hidden Glade

In the heart of the green, shadows play,
A whisper of light, in glimmering sway.
The secrets of nature, softly enfold,
In a hush of the night, their magic unfolds.

Crickets sing low, the moon takes its throne,
Silver beams dance where the wildflowers groan.
Each step a ripple, a spark in the dark,
Guiding the wanderer, igniting the spark.

Beneath ancient boughs, the stillness persists,
Voices of nature, in soft, gentle mists.
Starlight drips down like dew on the grass,
Time slows its pace, moments tenderly pass.

A flicker, a breeze, a secretive wink,
In the glade's embrace, lost souls softly think.
The night hums a tune, forgotten and rare,
Cradling hearts in its soft, loving care.

Awakened by dreams, the dawn will arrive,
Yet treasures of night inspire us to thrive.
In the luminance bright, let us cherish and stay,
For the hidden glade gives night a soft sway.

Faery Gifts in Shadowed Boughs

In the quiet of woods, where shadows convene,
Faery whispers tumble, delicate and keen.
Beneath the great oaks, their laughter is found,
Gifts wrapped in moonlight, scattered around.

Petals shift softly, revealing the charm,
A shimmering glow, woven with calm.
Each breath in the grove, a story unfolds,
Of magic and wonder, centuries old.

The night is alive with the sway of the trees,
A dance of the fae, carried on the breeze.
Sparkling drops fall like stars from above,
Nurturing dreams wrapped in feathers of love.

Branches entwined in a sweet, gentle maze,
Where time melts away in a mystical haze.
Shimmering treasures in the heart of the night,
Embodied through echoes, in soft, silver light.

So linger and breathe, in this hidden embrace,
Swap secrets with shadows, in this hallowed place.
The faery gifts waiting, they beckon and call,
In shadowed boughs' cradle, inviting us all.

Spirals of Light in the Verdant Dream

Through emerald fields, where the wild winds weave,
Spirals of light dance, in dreams we conceive.
From petals to leaves, a luminous thread,
A tapestry spun, where the heart's gently led.

Whispers of nature, a soft serenade,
The pulse of the earth, in twilight parade.
A flicker of hope, in the darkest of nights,
In spirals of light, the soul takes its flights.

Gentle the touch of the twilight's embrace,
In verdant realms, where we find our place.
Each step through the glade feels a magic divine,
As the stars ignite, in a celestial line.

In the hush of the evening, soft shadows will sway,
Threads of illumination to guide the way.
A symphony plays, under starlit skies,
Beneath the bright gaze of the moon's silver eyes.

So dream and believe, in the light that we share,
In spirals of hope, our hearts laid bare.
For within every gleam, a story unfolds,
In the depths of the night, there's magic it holds.

Dappled Whispers in Twilight's Realm

In twilight's embrace, whispers unfold,
Dappled in silence, mysteries told.
The colors of dusk weave a gentle lament,
As shadows connect, with a sweet, soft intent.

Leaves rustle lightly, a song on the air,
Unveiling the secrets that linger with care.
Each moment a brushstroke, painting the sky,
In twilight's soft glow, all worries fly high.

Glimmers of gold seep through branches entwined,
In this sanctuary, a haven defined.
Footsteps forgotten, in paths yet to roam,
Where echoes of magic feel endlessly home.

The stars come alive, a thousand-eyed gaze,
Reflecting the dreams, in a silvery haze.
Each twinkle a promise, each glow a caress,
In twilight's warm arms, we find our rest.

So linger and breathe, in this sacred domain,
Dappled whispers decide as they dance through the rain.
In the twilight's embrace, let our spirits entwine,
For every soft sigh knows the stars align.

Veils of Time in the Sylvan Grove

In shadows deep where whispers dwell,
The ancient trees weave tales to tell.
Time drapes its veils, both soft and light,
In the sylvan grove, a timeless night.

The moonbeams dance on emerald leaves,
As heartbeats echo through winding eves.
Lost in reverie, dreams take flight,
Veils of time shimmer in the night.

Echoes of laughter, soft and clear,
Fleeting moments held so dear.
Nature's breath, a gentle sigh,
In this sacred space we fly.

Beneath the boughs, memories swirl,
A tapestry rich, where shadows twirl.
Here in this grove, we come alive,
In veils of time, our souls revive.

Listen close, the trees will share,
Secrets of life, beyond compare.
Through every rustle, a story unfolds,
In the sylvan grove, where time beholds.

Silken Reveries of Nature's Breath

Amidst the blooms where whispers glide,
Nature's breath in silken tide.
Petals unfurl, soft as a dream,
In tranquil realms, we gently beam.

Golden rays through blossoms shine,
Each moment crafted, pure, divine.
The rustling leaves compose a tune,
In silken reveries of bright June.

Butterflies flit on gossamer wings,
Carrying laughter that nature sings.
The fragrance lingers, sweet and mild,
In the embrace of the earth, so wild.

Reflections dance upon the brook,
In every crevice, a secret nook.
With every breath, the world expands,
In silken dreams where beauty stands.

Awakening echoes, hear their call,
Through every whisper, we stand tall.
In nature's arms, we are reborn,
Silken reveries at the dawn.

The Dance of Petal-Laced Spirits

In gardens lush, where magic plays,
Petal-laced spirits weave through days.
With gentle grace, they twirl and spin,
In nature's heart, where dreams begin.

Beneath the boughs, in twilight's glow,
Whispers of beauty start to flow.
A tapestry rich, in colors bright,
The dance of spirits takes its flight.

Each bloom unfolds with secrets sweet,
Where earth and sky in harmony meet.
In the murmurs of the evening breeze,
Petal-laced spirits dance with ease.

Sunset glimmers on dewdrop cries,
As twilight deepens, the magic flies.
In every flutter, a tale to share,
The dance of spirits fills the air.

Through moonlit paths where shadows play,
Their laughter echoes, bright as day.
In every bloom, their essence spins,
The dance of life, where love begins.

Ethereal Patterns Beneath the Moon

When silver light adorns the night,
Ethereal patterns take their flight.
In whispered sighs, the stars align,
Beneath the moon, where spirits shine.

Clouds drift softly, a silken veil,
Carrying tales of winds that sail.
Each night a canvas, drawn anew,
In patterns ethereal, dreams break through.

The river's shimmer, a glistening flow,
Reflecting stories of hearts aglow.
In the stillness, the world unwinds,
Beneath the moon, our fate entwines.

Whispers of night in a tender breeze,
Stirring the leaves of ancient trees.
Guiding our paths through the darkened gloom,
Ethereal patterns beneath the moon.

In this twilight, souls become one,
Under the watch of the silver sun.
With every glow, our fears dissipate,
Embracing the night, we celebrate.

Echoes of the Otherworldly Garden

In whispers soft where shadows dwell,
Flowers bloom with tales to tell.
Moonlight weaves through emerald leaves,
Breath of night the darkness weaves.

Secrets held in every petal,
Fables sung in fragrant nettle.
Time stands still as stars align,
Echoes dance in blooms divine.

A symphony of rustling trees,
Nature's voice upon the breeze.
The heart beats with a tranquil sound,
In this garden, peace is found.

Among the roots, the spirits glide,
In the night where dreams reside.
Every hush a story spun,
In the glow of the evening sun.

Echoes linger, softly sigh,
In this realm where hopes can fly.
Through the dark, the light will guide,
In the garden, love abides.

Fragments of Stardust in the Canopy

High above where comets gleam,
Stars cascade in a golden stream.
Whispers float on winds so bright,
Fragments of magic in the night.

The leaves reflect a cosmic glow,
Ancient tales that trees can know.
In branches curled, the stories play,
Bright stardust dreams in soft array.

Night creeps in with velvet grace,
The universe found in this space.
Songs of old, the heavens hum,
In the quiet, the cosmos drum.

Glimmers dance in twinkling light,
A tapestry of dreams in flight.
Each soft rustle, a hymn retold,
Fragments of stardust, pure and bold.

In the shadows where truth mixes,
Life's bright song, each heart intermixes.
Within the canopy's embrace,
We find our home, our sacred place.

The Secret Symphony of Celestial Threads

In the cosmos where moments blend,
Celestial threads twist and wend.
With each note, the heavens sigh,
A symphony beneath the sky.

Stars are strings on a harp of night,
Plucked by dreams that take their flight.
The melodies weave through time and space,
Binding all in an endless embrace.

Hearts beat in rhythm, soft and low,
Each heartbeat sends a wave aglow.
The secrets whisper on the breeze,
Carried far through ancient trees.

Galaxies spin and dance apart,
Each movement is a work of art.
In the silence between each breath,
Lies the sound of life and death.

Listen close; let your spirit soar,
In this symphony, forever more.
Celestial threads unite us all,
In the cosmic dance, we rise, we fall.

Dance of the Enchanted Filaments

In twilight's glow, the filaments sway,
A dance of light that finds its way.
Threads of magic twist and spin,
Inviting dreams to breathe within.

Whispers float through the dusky air,
With every swirl, release your care.
The world ignites in colors bright,
As shadows mingle with the light.

The dance unfolds beneath the stars,
Enchanted dreams from near and far.
With every step, the spirits play,
In this waltz of night and day.

Boundless joy in simple grace,
Each movement, an embrace of space.
In the rhythm where hearts unite,
A tapestry of pure delight.

So take my hand and spin around,
In this dance, our souls are bound.
With every filament that we trace,
The universe reveals its face.

Whispers of Gossamer Dreams

In the hush of night, they sing,
Softly weaving through the air,
Gentle echoes, fragile wings,
Carrying wishes everywhere.

Fleeting moments, like the dew,
Kissed by dawn's first golden light,
Each dream a promise born anew,
Dancing shadows, taking flight.

With every sigh, a story spins,
Threads of hope entwined with fear,
Lost and found, as silence wins,
Dust of stars, forever near.

Whispers linger, hearts awake,
Breath of magic fills the seams,
In the silence, dreams will break,
Building worlds from shattered dreams.

So let the gossamer weave us tight,
Through every night and blushing dawn,
Together wrapped in dreams so light,
While time holds still, and we move on.

Enchanted Threads of Twilight

Underneath the twilight glow,
Threads of silver, spun from night,
Stitch the sky with fading show,
Crafting tales of pure delight.

Whispers flow on gentle breeze,
Carrying secrets, soft and sweet,
Where the heart finds quiet ease,
And the day and night both meet.

In the tapestry of dreams,
Merging dark with hints of light,
Time unravels at the seams,
Freed beneath the stars so bright.

Each horizon, a promise clear,
Woven in hues of deep embrace,
In this moment, have no fear,
For dreams are waiting, time and space.

So let us dance in twilight's fold,
Wrap ourselves in magic's thread,
Stories waiting to be told,
As night's sweet journey lays ahead.

Celestial Woven Fantasies

Night unfolds a tapestry,
Stars twinkle in their dance,
A cosmic show, wild and free,
Inviting us to take a chance.

In the silence of the sky,
Fantasies begin to bloom,
Weaving dreams that soar and fly,
Slicing through the velvet gloom.

Galaxies spill their glowing light,
Spiraling in a timeless spin,
Unraveling the heart's delight,
As we let our journey begin.

Connected by the threads of fate,
Every heartbeat finds its place,
Woven stories, love innate,
Every moment filled with grace.

So reach for stars, let wishes soar,
In the bounds of fate's embrace,
In celestial dreams we explore,
Finding hope in time and space.

Veils of Starlit Mystery

Beneath the cloak of midnight's veil,
Mysteries linger in the air,
Silent whispers tell a tale,
Of secrets woven with great care.

Veils that shimmer, cloaked in light,
Hiding wonders deep inside,
Diaphanous dreams take to flight,
In every shadow hope resides.

Twinkling stars, a guiding hand,
Leading hearts through the unknown,
In the depths where dreams expand,
Finding the magic all our own.

With each breath, a story shared,
Of love, loss, and journeys grand,
In the night, we're gently bared,
Bound by fate's invisible strand.

So let the starlit mystery soar,
Into realms where dreams align,
In every heart, a hidden door,
Awaiting truth that sparkles, shines.

Dreamlike Woven Echoes in Twilight's Embrace

In twilight's hush, the echoes creep,
Whispers of dreams in shadows deep.
Stars wink softly, time's gentle gaze,
Woven moments in a dusky haze.

Misty meadows where wonders blend,
Thoughts like whispers, they twist and bend.
The moon casts silver, a fleeting guide,
On paths where hidden dreams reside.

In dreamlike sways, the night takes flight,
Enchanting hues in fading light.
Hearts entwined in a velvet dance,
Lost in moments, a perfect chance.

Fragrant breezes whisper low,
Soft melodies in twilight flow.
Each sigh of night with secrets wrapped,
In twilight's embrace, we are entrapped.

A canvas strewn with starlit grace,
In these echoes, we find our place.
Through dreamlike realms we stroll and roam,
In twilight's weave, we find our home.

Nature's Palette in the Faerie Light

In glades where sunlight dances bright,
Nature paints in faerie light.
Petals twinkle, colors sing,
A vibrant hush that joys can bring.

Emerald leaves with gold entwined,
Whispers of breeze, so sweet and kind.
Beneath the bows, the faeries play,
In nature's arms, they weave the day.

Crimson berries, sapphire skies,
Every hue a soft surprise.
Mossy carpets, whispers low,
In this realm, pure wonders flow.

Silken threads of sunbeam's thread,
Through tranquil woods, our spirits tread.
With every shade, a tale unfolds,
In nature's heart, a joy retold.

As twilight drapes its gentle grace,
Nature's palette finds its place.
In every leaf, in every light,
The faerie world ignites the night.

Enigmatic Traces of the Sylvan Spirits

In forests deep, where shadows play,
Sylvan spirits dance and sway.
Echoes of laughter in the trees,
Whispers carried on the breeze.

Moonlit paths with secrets shared,
Footsteps soft where few have dared.
Traces left in dew-kissed glades,
Mystic traces, nature's shades.

Cloaked in twilight's gentle cloak,
Voices rise, a soft-spun spoke.
In every rustle, a tale resides,
Of ancient lore where magic hides.

Through towering oaks and silver birch,
The spirits stir, a rhythmic search.
Their enigmatic breath, a balm,
In sylvan halls that whisper calm.

Each flicker, a promise of the night,
Sylvan spirits imbued with light.
In every corner, secrets sleep,
In nature's heart, our souls we keep.

Captivating Shadows Among the Orchard Trees

Beneath the trees where shadows quilt,
In fragrant air, our hearts are built.
Apples blush in golden glow,
Captivating whispers in the flow.

Rustling leaves and gentle sighs,
Dance along as daylight dies.
In twilight's fold, a secret grace,
Among the trees, we find our place.

Softly golden, the evening spills,
Filling air with sweetened thrills.
Shadows play in hues of dusk,
In this orchard, life is husk.

Footsteps echo in the night,
Underneath the stars so bright.
And every glance, a story told,
As moonlight weaves with threads of gold.

The orchard keeps its mysteries near,
In shadows deep, we've nothing to fear.
Together here, we share our dreams,
Among the trees, life softly beams.

Wisps of Magic in the Grove

In the twilight hour, shadows play,
Whispers of secrets, soft and gray.
Leaves shimmer bright, like stars above,
Nature's embrace, a tender love.

Crisp air sighs, the night unfolds,
Tales of enchantment, gently told.
Footsteps wander through misty trails,
Where every heartbeat softly pales.

Glimmers of hope weave through the night,
Dreams take flight in silver light.
Rustling branches serenade the soul,
While owls keep watch, their eyes so whole.

Mushrooms glow with a magic spark,
Drawing explorers into the dark.
Fairies dance on the emerald ground,
In this hidden realm, joy is found.

Forest Spirits and Gossamer Veils

Amid the trees, where spirits dwell,
A tapestry of secrets swell.
Whispers of wind in the ancient oaks,
In a world alive with timeless strokes.

Gossamer veils hang like dreams,
Softly spun from silvered beams.
The forest breathes, a gentle sigh,
As magic flutters and laughter flies.

Crickets sing in the cooling dusk,
Nature's rhythm, rich and plush.
Moonlight dances on tranquil streams,
Awakening the landscape's dreams.

Each rustle speaks of hidden grace,
In this woodland, a sacred space.
Let your heart wander, gently roam,
For in this realm, you'll find your home.

Tread Lightly in the Glimmering Glade

Glimmers flicker on the dewy grass,
A delicate touch as fairies pass.
Tread lightly here, where magic thrives,
In the heart of nature, the spirit survives.

Crimson blooms and emerald leaves,
Whispering tales of what one believes.
Beneath the boughs, a soft light gleams,
Awakening every hidden dream.

A chorus of crickets sings the night,
Guiding the lost towards the light.
In the glade, under a silvery dome,
The essence of magic finds its home.

Here in the quiet, the world stands still,
Nature's enchantment, a soothing thrill.
With every breath, let wonder flow,
In this sacred space, let your spirit grow.

Celestial Embroidery of the Glimmering Wood

Stars above weave an intricate lace,
And grace the woods with a gentle trace.
Each night unfolds tales spun in light,
Under the canopy, dreams take flight.

Moonbeams dance on the forest floor,
Painting stories to explore.
Each rustling leaf holds a tale untold,
In whispers soft, in shades of gold.

Be careful where your footsteps lead,
For every spirit hears your creed.
In the magic of shadows, they reside,
Guardian spirits, with hearts open wide.

A canvas of stars, a celestial blend,
In this enchanted grove, time may bend.
With every heartbeat, the woods ignite,
In the embroidery of the eternal night.

Ghostly Tracings on a Faery Path

Whispers echo through the trees,
Footprints vanish with the breeze.
Shimmering lights dance in the night,
Guiding dreams with soft delight.

Misty fog cloaks ancient trails,
Secrets bound in hidden veils.
Each step taken feels like fate,
In a realm where time won't wait.

Silvery shadows flit and play,
Leading wanderers lost away.
Underneath the starlit skies,
The magic deepens, never dies.

Echoing laughter, soft and sweet,
A promise lies beneath our feet.
Through the garden, wild and free,
The past and future's mystery.

Night reveals its fabled lore,
With every step, we yearn for more.
Ghostly tracings on this path,
Awake the heart, ignite the wrath.

Captured Fragments of Enchanted Flight

Wings unfurl in dazzling arcs,
Carrying dreams through twilight sparks.
Tender whispers, soft as sighs,
Capture magic in the skies.

Fleeting moments turn to light,
Hovering in the air, so slight.
Fragile flutters, brief yet bold,
Threads of wonder softly told.

Every glimpse a treasure rare,
Lost in time, yet always there.
The heart takes flight with stories spun,
By gossamer trails, the journey's begun.

In those fragments, dreams collide,
Carried forth by winds that guide.
Essence captured, bold and bright,
In the dance of pure delight.

Each fleeting fragment, wings of grace,
Whispers linger in empty space.
Fragments of an enchanted flight,
Lost in starlight, taking flight.

The Stitched Chronicles of Fairyland

In hidden nooks, the stories dwell,
Tales of magic, woven well.
Threads of stardust, dreams entwined,
In a tapestry of the divine.

With needle sharp, the tales unfold,
Of brave hearts and treasures bold.
Each stitch a secret, rich and deep,
The chronicles that time must keep.

Pages flutter like wings above,
Whispers linger, tales of love.
Bound in laughter, stitched with tears,
Carrying hopes throughout the years.

In glades where sunlight softly plays,
The stories echo in gentle ways.
An ancient book, forever grand,
The stitched chronicles of Fairyland.

With each new tale, a world reborn,
In hearts and dreams, promise is sworn.
Timeless wonders woven tight,
In the fabric of the night.

Serenade of Gossamer Wings

A serenade drifts on the breeze,
Softly sung through rustling leaves.
Gossamer wings in moonlight's glow,
Tune of magic, sweet and low.

Melodies of twilight's charm,
Lull the night, embrace the calm.
Each note dances, light yet clear,
Inviting dreams to linger near.

In the whisper of the air,
Hopes and wishes, free from care.
Gossamer moments take their flight,
Carrying hearts through the night.

With every flutter, echoes rise,
Stories penned in starlit skies.
A serenade to the unseen,
In a realm both wild and serene.

Night blooms bright with enchanted song,
Wings of wonder guiding along.
In the softness, magic stings,
Echoed in the serenade of wings.

Echoes of Luminous Stitches

In twilight's embrace, the stars alight,
Threads of silver dance, igniting the night.
Whispers of dreams weave tales anew,
In the quiet of shadows, their magic is true.

With each gentle pulse, the fabric does sing,
A tapestry spun from the joys of the spring.
Colors collide in a joyous parade,
Echoes of laughter in memories made.

Stitches of time, both fragile and bold,
Each one a story that longs to be told.
Frayed edges soften, embrace of the past,
Luminous whispers, a bond built to last.

In the heart of the night, the needle takes flight,
Connecting our souls in the warmth of the light.
Threads intertwine, a delicate dance,
In this mosaic of life, we find our chance.

As dawn creeps near, and shadows grow long,
The echoes of stitches sing a sweet song.
In the quilt of existence, we find our place,
A radiant patchwork, filled with grace.

The Sylvan Canopy's Embrace

Beneath the great trees, in dappled green,
Whispers of nature, a tranquil scene.
Sunlight filters softly through leaves above,
In the sylvan embrace, we find our love.

The breeze rustles gently, a sweet serenade,
Telling tales of the forest, in shadows and shade.
Moss carpets the ground, a plush, inviting bed,
Where dreams intertwine, where our hearts are led.

Branches stretch outward, an arching embrace,
A sanctuary found in this sacred space.
Birdsong surrounds us, a chorus of cheer,
In the whispers of foliage, we hold each other near.

The canopy sways as the seasons unfold,
In hues of deep green, red, and gold.
Every rustle and sigh, a love story spun,
In the heart of the forest, where time comes undone.

With each step we take on this enchanted ground,
In the magic of woods, our souls are unbound.
Together we wander, forever entwined,
In the sylvan embrace, true peace we find.

Fluttering Secrets in a Hidden Grove

In a hidden grove where secrets reside,
Fluttering wings whisper tales far and wide.
Petals unfold, revealing their hearts,
Nature's soft brush, where magic imparts.

Dappled sunlight dances on leaves overhead,
As whispers of breezes weave dreams through the bed.
Butterflies flit, with colors so bright,
Guardians of secrets held tight in the night.

Amidst the lush ferns, a soft sigh is heard,
The language of silence, unspoken, inferred.
In stillness, we listen, the heartbeat of earth,
The fluttering secrets that promise rebirth.

Moonlight cascades through the branches above,
Kissing the grove with a tender, soft love.
In the night's gentle hush, we hear the refrain,
Of fluttering secrets that shimmer like rain.

With every lost whisper, a mystery swells,
In the verdant embrace, where enchantment dwells.
We gather these secrets, as night dances on,
In the heart of the grove, where our spirits are drawn.

Translucent Whispers in the Garden of Spirits

In the garden of spirits, where shadows play,
Translucent whispers guide the lost on their way.
Petals like ghosts in the soft morning mist,
Each breath we take holds an ethereal twist.

Crimson and ivory, colors softly blend,
Where the past and the present entwine and extend.
In silence they linger, these whispers so light,
Tracing the paths of the day and the night.

Figures of memory in the twilight appear,
Echoing echoes, both distant and near.
In the stillness of time, they beckon us close,
With translucent whispers, we honor the ghost.

Flowers bloom bravely in shades of the past,
In the garden of spirits, where moments are cast.
Each fragrance imbued with a tale to be told,
In the whispers of petals, their beauty unfolds.

With every soft rustle, a message flows through,
In the heart of the garden, our spirits renew.
Translucent and tender, the bonds never sever,
In the garden of spirits, we linger forever.

www.ingramcontent.com/pod-product-compliance
Ingram Content Group UK Ltd.
Pitfield, Milton Keynes, MK11 3LW, UK
UKHW021434160125
4146UKWH00006B/87

9 781805 594505